# THE AMAZING BOOK OF FIRST
# INVENTIONS

# THE AMAZING BOOK OF FIRSTS
# INVENTIONS

Written by David Smith & Sue Cassin
Illustrated by Kim Blundell

Edited by Catriona Macgregor

**COLLINS**

# CONTENTS

### MAN-MADE MATERIALS
### p. 6-7

Essential inventions of man-made materials, including nylon, glass and concrete.

### INSTRUMENTS FOR MEASURING
### p. 8-9

The first time for the clock, the speedometer and other measuring marvels.

### MACHINES
### p. 10-11

The original elevator, the bulldozer, and other amazing machine inventions.

### ROADS, BRIDGES AND CANALS
### p. 12-13

The origins of these common constructions, including an ancient Egyptian dam, a Roman bridge and a royal underwater tunnel.

### BUILDINGS
### p. 14-15

Building brainwaves, such as the first house, skyscraper, hotel and supermarket.

### SAFETY
### p. 16-17

Fire escapes, parachutes and lifeboats are amongst vital inventions in this safety section.

### POWER AND ENERGY
### p. 18-19

Find out about the eighteenth-century solar panel, the volcano-heated swimming pool and the first ever windmill!

### COMMUNICATIONS
### p. 20-21

The first postman, satellite, typewriter and phone call come in this communications category.

## HI-TECH
## p. 22–23

First from the world of hi-tech science, including the credit card-sized radio and the world's most accurate clock.

## MUSICAL INSTRUMENTS
## p. 24–25

A musical medley, with pottery drums, prehistoric pipes and musical coconuts!

## MEDICINE
## p. 26–27

A selection of medical firsts, including the first thermometer, x-ray and stethoscope.

## WHACKY INVENTIONS
## p. 28–29

Some strange, one-off inventions which never worked, including the chocolate medicine spoon, the edible record and the bird-powered balloon!

# MAN-MADE MATERIALS

**CLAY CITY**—The oldest known bricks are those which were used to build the city of Jericho in Jordan in about 6000 BC. The bricks themselves were made from clay, reinforced with straw and baked in the sun.

The first brick-making machine was built in 1839 by Messrs Cooke and Cunningham of Great Britain. The machine could make as many as 18,000 bricks in ten hours.

**CONCRETE TEMPLE**—The first known use of concrete was in the lining of an aqueduct which was built in about 700 BC in Jerwan in Iraq.

The first concrete building was the Temple of Concord, built in 121 BC in Rome.

**GLASS FIRST**—Glass was first made in 3000 BC in the Middle East by melting together sand and soda. By the first century BC Syrians were using blowpipes to make glass vessels, but it was over 1,000 years before flat glass was first in use—it appeared in Europe around AD 1300.

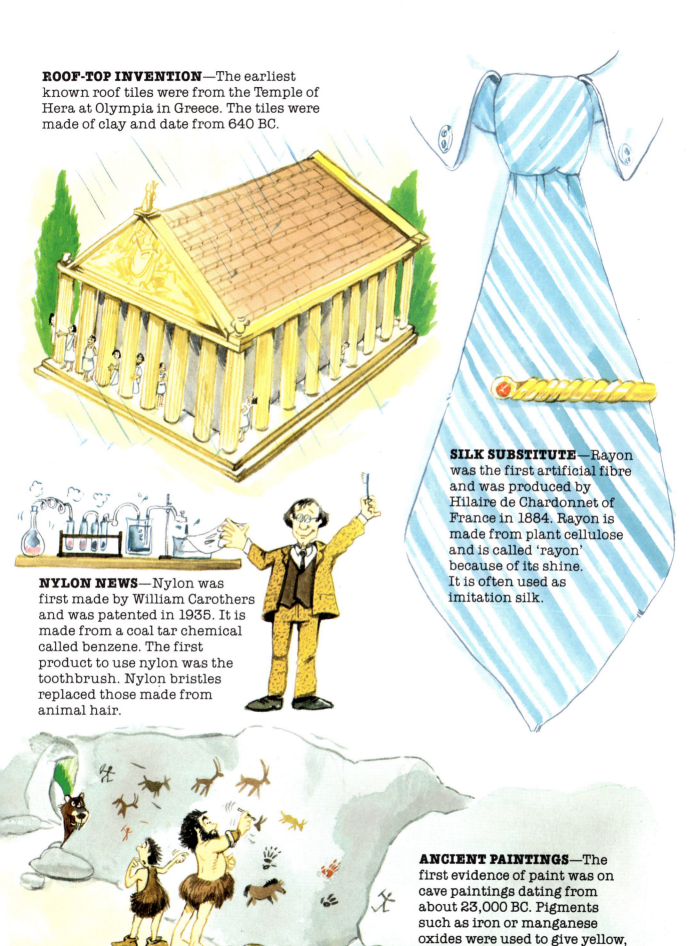

**ROOF-TOP INVENTION**—The earliest known roof tiles were from the Temple of Hera at Olympia in Greece. The tiles were made of clay and date from 640 BC.

**SILK SUBSTITUTE**—Rayon was the first artificial fibre and was produced by Hilaire de Chardonnet of France in 1884. Rayon is made from plant cellulose and is called 'rayon' because of its shine. It is often used as imitation silk.

**NYLON NEWS**—Nylon was first made by William Carothers and was patented in 1935. It is made from a coal tar chemical called benzene. The first product to use nylon was the toothbrush. Nylon bristles replaced those made from animal hair.

**ANCIENT PAINTINGS**—The first evidence of paint was on cave paintings dating from about 23,000 BC. Pigments such as iron or manganese oxides were used to give yellow, red and black colours.

# INSTRUMENTS FOR MEASURING

**EGYPTIAN MEASUREMENT**—In about 3000 BC the Egyptians used the 'cubit'—a measurement of about 46cm. It was the distance from the elbow to the tip of the middle finger.

**METRIC MEASUREMENT**—In 1793 the French National Assembly began the metric system. The metre was defined as one ten-millionth of the distance from the North Pole to the Equator.

**ITALIAN IDEA**—In Italy in 1593 Galileo Galilei designed a thermoscope to measure the temperature of the air.

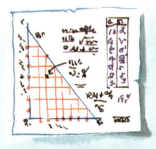

**CLOCK FIRST**—The Egyptians were the first people to use a device for measuring time. As early as 2000 BC they were using a shadow clock.

**ASTRONOMER'S IDEA**—In 1742 Anders Celsius, a Swedish astronomer, introduced the centigrade scale. It is used for measuring temperature.

**WIND SPEED INSTRUMENTS**—In 1846 Thomas Robinson, an Irish astronomer, invented the four-cup anemometer—an instrument for measuring the speed of wind.

**ITALIAN INVENTION**—Barometers measure the pressure of the atmosphere around us. The first one was devised in 1643 by an Italian called Torricelli.

**ANCIENT RAIN GAUGE**—An early rain gauge was described in an Indian manuscript which dates back to 4000 BC. The rain gauge consisted of a bowl which measured the rainfall in a set period of time.

**SPEEDOMETER FIRST**—The first motor car speedometer was manufactured in 1910 by Thorpe and Salter Ltd of London. The instrument showed speeds of 0–35 mph.

# MACHINES

**TELE-MOLE TUNNELLER**—The first tunnelling machine was devised in 1818 by Marc Isambard Brunel. He designed the first machine for tunnelling under the River Thames.

The first fully automatic tunnelling machine, called the 'Tele-Mole', was developed in the 1970s in Japan. It is controlled from the surface and the operator keeps it on course by aiming a laser beam through a 'gun-sight' which can be seen on a TV screen.

**MIXING MACHINE**—The first concrete mixer was used in 1857 for building a bridge over the River Tisza at Szeged in Hungary.

**STEAM ENGINE CONVERSION**—In 1923 Benjamin Holt invented the first bulldozer. He fitted caterpillar tracks to a steam traction engine and attached a special blade to the front of the machine.

**SNOW STORM INVENTION**—The first snow plough for clearing railway lines was built in 1883 by Leslie Brothers of Orangeville in Ontario. It was tested by the Canadian Pacific Railway.

**ARCHITECT'S IDEA**—In 10 BC a Roman architect called Vitruvius described the first crane. It was said to consist of a strong pole with a pulley at the top, held in position by ropes.

**LAZY SHOPPER'S SOLUTION**—In 1857 the Otis Steam Elevator Company of the USA fitted the first passenger elevator. It was installed in a shop in New York City and carried about six people. This invention encouraged the building of skyscrapers.

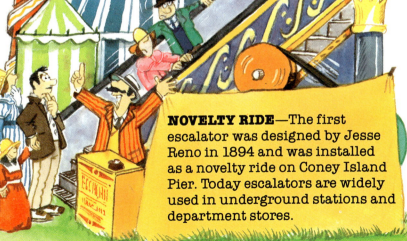

**NOVELTY RIDE**—The first escalator was designed by Jesse Reno in 1894 and was installed as a novelty ride on Coney Island Pier. Today escalators are widely used in underground stations and department stores.

# ROADS, BRIDGES AND CANALS

**FIRST ROADS**—The Romans began building the first proper roads throughout their Empire in about 350 BC. For materials they used stone slabs on top of smaller stone in mortar. The surface of the road was slightly curved to allow water to drain away on either side of the road.

In the 18th century, after years of neglect, road conditions began to improve dramatically with the efforts of John Macadam and Pierre Trésaguet.

**ROMAN BRIDGE**—The first stone bridge was built in 142 BC by Roman engineers. It spanned the River Tiber in Rome.

**BOLTLESS BRIDGE**—The first iron bridge was built in 1779 by Abraham Darby. It stretches across the River Severn at Telford in England. Believe it or not, not one screw, rivet, nut or bolt was used—the bridge is held together only by perfect dovetail joints.

**RIVER LINKS**—The very first canals were built in about 4000 BC in Mesopotamia. They linked rivers together and so helped to improve irrigation.

The first long canal, the Grand Canal, was built in China. It was begun in 600 BC and by AD 1327 it had grown into a canal system which was 1,782km long. At one period in its construction a total of 5 million people were working on it! The Grand Canal is still in use today.

**EGYPTIAN DAM**—The oldest known dam was built between 2950 and 2750 BC by the Ancient Egyptians. It spanned the Garawi valley and contained about 100,000 tonnes of earth faced with stone. Its base was 84m thick. The dam only lasted a few years before the weight of the water behind it burst the wall.

**PALACE TUNNEL**—The first underwater tunnel was built in 2160 BC in Babylon, Mesopotamia, and ran under the River Euphrates. During the dry season the river was diverted in order to allow the engineers to build a 900m long brick-lined tunnel in the river bed. This connected Queen Semirani's palace with a temple across the river.

# BUILDINGS

**TALL STORY**—The first skyscraper was the 10-storey Home Insurance Company building in Chicago. The 52m-high building was designed by William Le Baron Jenny and its construction was completed in 1882.

**GOOD FOOD**—Low's Grand Hotel in Covent Garden, London was the first hotel ever. It opened in 1774 and soon became known for its high-quality food.

**SUPERMARKET STARTER**—An American called Michael Cullen started the first supermarket, on Long Island. It opened in 1930 and was known as 'King Kullen Food Stores'.

**SHOPPING PALACE**—The Marble Dry Goods Palace on Broadway, New York City was the first department store. It was opened by Alexander Turney Stewart in 1848 and, at that time, was the largest shop in the World!

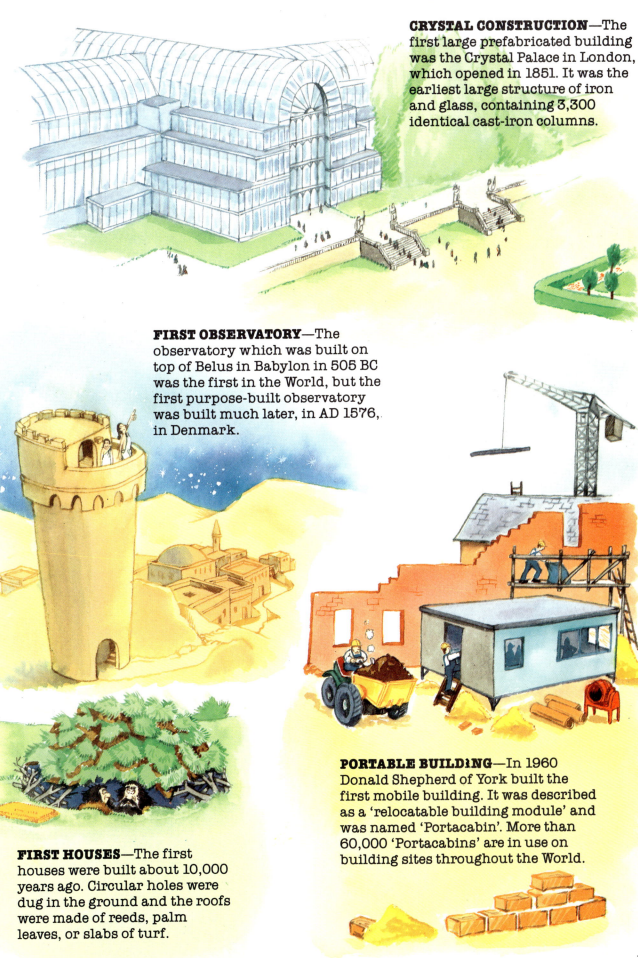

**CRYSTAL CONSTRUCTION**—The first large prefabricated building was the Crystal Palace in London, which opened in 1851. It was the earliest large structure of iron and glass, containing 3,300 identical cast-iron columns.

**FIRST OBSERVATORY**—The observatory which was built on top of Belus in Babylon in 505 BC was the first in the World, but the first purpose-built observatory was built much later, in AD 1576, in Denmark.

**PORTABLE BUILDING**—In 1960 Donald Shepherd of York built the first mobile building. It was described as a 'relocatable building module' and was named 'Portacabin'. More than 60,000 'Portacabins' are in use on building sites throughout the World.

**FIRST HOUSES**—The first houses were built about 10,000 years ago. Circular holes were dug in the ground and the roofs were made of reeds, palm leaves, or slabs of turf.

# SAFETY

**LIFEBOAT LAUNCH**—The very first lifeboat was launched in 1790 from South Shields in North East England. The boat was called *Original* and was in service for a total of 40 years.

**SEAT BELT SECURITY**—In 1959 seat belts were fitted to a car for the first time. The car was a production model of a Swedish-made Volvo.

**CAR CAUTION**—Road users in London were the first to be stopped by traffic lights. The lights were built on top of 6.6m cast-iron pillars and came into operation in December 1868. They had red and green signals and were lit by gas. The lantern was operated by a policeman who turned a lever at the base.

**LUCKY CAT**—Cat's eyes—reflecting road studs which help motorists to see the middle of the road in dark or foggy conditions—were invented in 1934 by an English road repairer called Percy Shaw. Whilst driving in the dark, he noticed the glinting eyes of a cat sitting on a fence. This prevented him from crashing through the fence and falling down a sheer drop.

**FLAME FIGHTER**—The first fire-extinguisher was invented in 1734 by a Mr Fuches of Germany. It consisted of water-filled glass balls which were thrown onto the fire.

In 1816 George Manby of Yarmouth introduced the first modern automatic fire-extinguisher. This extinguisher was a 30cm high copper cylinder filled with a mixture of water, pearl ash and compressed air.

**FLYING PILOT**—The first aircraft to be fitted with an ejection seat was a Junkers 88. The seat was fitted in 1939 and by the following year 200 test ejections had been made.

**BRAVE BALLOONIST**—André Jacques Garnerin, a balloon inspector in the French Army, was the first person ever to make a parachute descent. In 1797 he jumped from a balloon above Paris at a height of 680m.

**WATCHMAKER'S ESCAPE**—Believe it or not, the first fire-escape was invented in 1766 by a London watchmaker. It was a simple apparatus consisting of a wicker basket on a pulley and chain.

# POWER AND ENERGY

**FACTORY FIRST**—The first tidal power station was called the Usine Marémotrice de la Rance and was opened in 1968 at the estuary of the River Rance in the Gulf of St Malo. The station took fiv years to build, and now produces 544 million kilowatts of electricity each year.

**SOLAR ENERGY**—The simplest way to tap the Sun's power is to collect its heat. In the 18th century Horace-Bénédict de Saussure, a Swiss scientist, designed the first solar heating panel. The panel can reach a temperature of up to 88°C.

**NUCLEAR-POWERED TOWN**—The first nuclear power station was built at Obninsk, USSR and began producing electricity in 1954. It supplied enough electricity for a town of 6,000 people.

**ANCIENT WINDMILL**—In AD 644 the Persians were the first to provide power to grind corn, but the first windmill which actually generated electricity appeared in Denmark in 1890. A M. la Cour fitted patent sails and twin fantails onto a steel tower.

**ICY SWIM**—The first power station to use the geothermal energy, from the heat stored in the Earth's core, was built in Tuscany, Italy.

Another of the first countries to tap the Earth's heat was Iceland. Engineers use this heat by piping hot water from underground to warm nearby houses, offices, and factories. In Iceland's capital, Reykjavik, an outdoor swimming pool is heated this way, all year round!

**WATER WONDER**—The first hydro-electric power stations were built in 1891 near Frankfurt, and at the Niagara Falls. The power is produced by water-driven turbines and, believe it or not, generates 25% of the World's electricity!

# COMMUNICATIONS

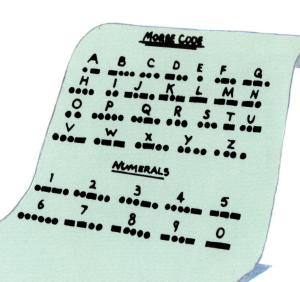

**CRYPTIC CODE**—Morse code was introduced in 1838 by Samuel Morse from the USA. The code consists of patterns of shorts dots and long dashes which indicate the letters of the alphabet.

**LONG-DISTANCE LINE**—The first telephone was displayed to the public in Philadelphia in 1876. It was patented by Alexander Graham Bell, a Scottish-born inventor, and it contained the first microphone.

In 1884 the Bell Telephone Company of the USA set up the first ever long-distance telephone line. 1927 saw the first transatlantic telephone links—between New York and London.

**TRANSATLANTIC TELEVISION**—The first transatlantic live TV satellite transmission was via 'Telstar' between Andover, Maine and Goonhilly Downs, in Cornwall, in 1962.

**MOON TRANSMISSION**—By 1965 a total of 300 million viewers in 9 countries were able to watch TV programmes via the 'Early Bird' satellite. A year later 'Luna 9', an unmanned space probe, landed on the Moon and sent TV pictures back to Earth.

**WEATHER REPORT**—The first satellite to provide useful weather information was the American satellite, 'Tiros 1'.

**TYPEWRITER FIRST**—In 1874 Christopher Scholes and Carlos Glidden from the USA produced the first modern typewriter. In 1902 the first successful electric typewriter was sold by the Blickensdorfer Company of the USA.

**FIRST POSTMAN**—In 1664 King Louis XI of France set up a state postal service—the first since the Roman Empire. Mail was delivered by messengers on horseback.

**FLYING LETTERS**—The world's first regular airmail service began in the UK in 1911. Bags of letters were carried to Europe by aeroplane from London.

# HI-TEC

**GIANT CALCULATOR**—In 1945 two Americans called Presper Eckert and John Maunchly designed the first fully-electronic computer. It was more like a giant calculator than a computer as it could not store data or programs.

**COMPACT CAMERA**—The first photographic camera was manufactured for sale and marketed by Alphonse Giroux of Paris in 1839.

In 1925 a German company called Leitz designed the first small hand-held camera.

**LASER FIRST**—In 1960 Theodore Maiman from the USA built a machine to make the first laser beams. Today, lasers are used for many different purposes, from surgical operations to cutting cloth.

**3-D INVENTION**—Holography is the technique of producing a three-dimensional photograph of an object by using laser beams. This was first demonstrated in 1963 by Emmett Leith and Juris Upatnieks of Michigan University.

In 1984 the American magazine, the *National Geographic*, was the first to show a hologram on its cover.

**SPECTACULAR MICROSCOPE**—In around 1590 two Dutch spectacle makers, Hans and Zacharias Janssen, made the first microscope. The lenses they used, however, were not very powerful and therefore did not produce a very accurate image.

In 1683 Antonie van Leeuwenhoek used a very powerful lens. This was so much more effective that, for the first time, bacteria could be seen. Not knowing what they were, van Leeuwenhoek described them as 'little animals'.

**ATOMIC ACCURACY**—In 1969 scientists from the US Naval Research Laboratory in Washington D.C. built the first ammonia atomic clock, which is so accurate that it would take 1,700,000 years for it to be one second out!

**LONG-DISTANCE LINE**—The first fibre optic telephone link was opened in 1977 in Hertfordshire. This enables thousands of telephone calls to be carried at the same time.

**ROBOTS' WORK**—The first industrial robots were made in the USA in 1962. They were the 'pick and place' type which were able to move objects around.

In the late 1970s robots began spot welding cars and spraying the bodywork with paint, and by 1983 Yamazaki of Japan were using robots to manufacture robots!

**TINY RADIO**—In 1985 Sony of Japan produced a miniature radio which was only 3mm thick! It was nicknamed the 'Credit Card Radio' because it was so thin.

# MUSICAL INSTRUMENTS

**PHILADELPHIAN PIANO**—The first piano was built in 1709 by Bartolomeo Cristofori of Florence. In 1800 John Hawkins from Philadelphia built the first upright piano.

**ANCIENT STRINGS**—The harp is the oldest instrument in the string section of the orchestra. It has been attributed to Jubal, son of Lamech and Adah (Genesis, Old Testament) since about 3875 BC.

**MUSICAL COCONUT**—The first ever reference to string instruments played with a bow appears in Persian and Chinese writings dating from about AD 800. The oldest known violin was an ancient instrument called a *kemantche*. It was played in Persia and consisted of a long stick which extended through half of a coconut.

**PERCUSSION PIECE**—The xylophone is said to have originated in South East Asia or Oceania. It was first mentioned in 1511 in Europe and was introduced into China from Burma at the end of the 18th century. The xylophone is one of the most important instruments in African Music and is also often used in the percussion section of an orchestra.

**PREHISTORIC MUSIC**—Bagpipes are a prehistoric instrument, first played in the Middle East and China. They were made from lamb or goatskin to which pipes were attached.

**PIPE PROGRESS**—The recorder was originally developed from prehistoric pipes, although the first reference to them appeared in 1388.

In 1690 a Mr Denner of Nuremburg invented the first clarinet as a further development of the recorder.

**JAZZ SOLO**—In 1846 a Belgian instrument maker called Antoine Joseph Sax patented the saxophone. It soon became a popular solo instrument and is widely used in jazz bands today.

**SPANISH SERENADE**—The guitar was developed from the ancient lute (a pear-shaped string instrument). It was brought to Europe by the Moors in the first century AD and became Spain's national instrument. It appeared in its present form in about 1750.

**TURKISH TUNES**—Two percussion instruments, the cymbals and the triangle, were developed from Turkish military bands of ancient times. They were first used in an orchestra in 1680.

**POTTERY DRUMS**—Believe it or not, the first drums were made of pottery and were in the shape of an hour glass, with animal skins tied over either end. Examples dating as far back as 4000 BC have been found in Bohemia and along the Upper Nile.

# MEDICINE

**STETHOSCOPE FIRST**—The first stethoscope was designed in 1816 by a Frenchman called René Laennec. Unlike the stethoscopes which are used today, it had only one ear-piece. The modern 'two-ear' stethoscope was designed by a Mr Camman of the USA in 1850.

**ITALIAN INVENTION**—In 1896 Dr Riva-Rocci of Italy designed the first practical instrument for measuring blood pressure—the sphygmomanometer. If a person's blood pressure is too high or too low, then their health can be affected.

**X-RAY DISCOVERY**—Wilhelm Röntgen of West Germany was the first to discover x-rays. X-rays enable doctors to see inside a patient's body without having to perform surgery.

**FIRST THERMOMETER**—The first thermometer for measuring body temperature was used in 1616 by Santorio Santorio of Italy. The first clinical thermometer was introduced over 200 years later in 1863 by a Mr Aitken of Great Britain.

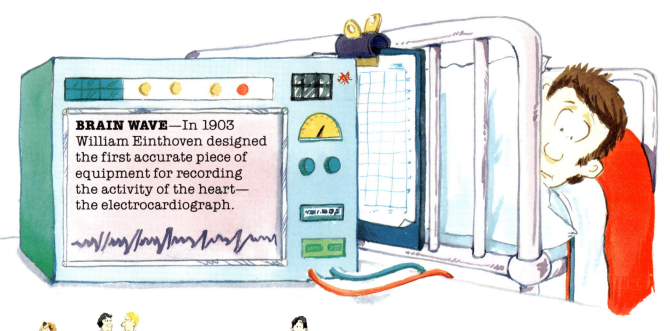

**BRAIN WAVE**—In 1903 William Einthoven designed the first accurate piece of equipment for recording the activity of the heart—the electrocardiograph.

**SCHOOL FOR DOCTORS**—The first medical school was to be found in Padua, Italy, in the 10th century.

**LADY DOCTOR**—The first woman doctor was Elizabeth Blackwell from England. She qualified in 1849 after studying medicine at the University of Geneva, New York State.

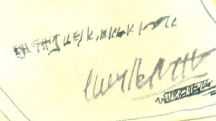

# WHACKY INVENTIONS

**BALLOON BIRDS**—In 1887 Charles Wulff of Paris produced an unusual design for a balloon. The power was to be supplied by large birds, such as eagles, which were to be tied to the framework of the machine.

**PLANE CALAMITY**—A Scottish engineer called Joseph Kaufmann patented his idea for an aeroplane in 1869. It consisted of a steam engine with wings which flapped like those of a bird. When he tried out a model of his extraordinary invention the wings flapped so violently that the whole machine fell to pieces!

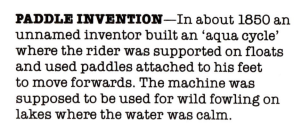

**PADDLE INVENTION**—In about 1850 an unnamed inventor built an 'aqua cycle' where the rider was supported on floats and used paddles attached to his feet to move forwards. The machine was supposed to be used for wild fowling on lakes where the water was calm.

**CLOCK SHOCK**—George Hogan of Chicago designed a unique alarm clock which wakened the sleeper by sending a stream of cold water down his or her neck!

**EDIBLE RECORDS**—A German company called Gebrüder Stollwerk was granted a patent in 1903 for a gramophone which played flat discs made of chocolate wrapped in tinfoil. After the records had been played they could be eaten!

**CHOCOLATE SPOON**—In 1937 Constance Honey of London patented a chocolate spoon for giving nasty medicine to children!

**MECHANICAL MAN**—Perhaps one of the most unusual inventions was patented in 1868 by Zadoc Dederick and Isaac Grass of New Jersey. It was a partly-wheeled vehicle built in the form of a mechanical man pulling a cart. Powered by a steam engine built inside his body, the mechanical man was supposed to walk forwards pulling the vehicle behind him!

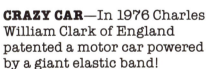

**CRAZY CAR**—In 1976 Charles William Clark of England patented a motor car powered by a giant elastic band!

**SNOWBALL STORY**—An Englishman called Arthur Paul Pedrick came up with an amazing idea to irrigate the Sahara Desert. His plan was to roll snowballs down a pipe from the North Pole. However, his scheme proved impractical and the pipe was never built.

# INDEX

airmail, 21

bagpipes, 25
barometers, 8
bricks, 6
bridges, 12
buildings 14-15
    hotels, 14
    houses, 15
    observatories, 15
    portable buildings, 15
    prefabricated buildings, 15
    skyscrapers, 14
bulldozers, 10

cameras, 22
canals, 13
cat's eyes, 16
clocks, 8
    atomic clocks, 23
computers, 22
concrete, 6
    concrete mixers, 10
cranes, 11

dams, 13
department stores, 14

ejection seats, 17
elevators, 11
escalators, 11

fire extinguishers, 17
fire-escapes, 17

glass, 6

holography, 22

lasers, 22
lifeboats, 16

measurements, 8-9
    blood pressure, 26
    heart activity, 27
    wind speed, 9
medical schools, 27
metric system, 8
microscopes, 23
miniature radios, 23

morse code, 20
musical instruments, 24-25
    cymbals, 25
    drums, 25
    harps, 24
    guitars, 25
    pianos, 24
    recorders, 25
    saxophones, 25
    triangles, 25
    violins, 24

nylon, 7

paint, 7
parachutes, 17
plastics, 7
postal service, 21
power stations, 18-19
    geothermal, 19
    hydro-electric, 19
    nuclear, 18
    tidal, 18

rain gauges, 9
roads, 12
robots, 23
roof tiles, 7

satellites, 20, 21
seat belts, 16
snow ploughs, 10
solar energy, 18
speedometers, 9
stethoscopes, 26
supermarkets, 14

telephones, 20
    fibre optic link, 23
temperature, 8
thermometers, 9, 26
traffic lights, 16
tunnelling machines, 10
typewriters, 21

whacky inventions, 28-29
windmills, 19

x-rays, 26
xylophones, 24